REV FRANCK J. DUMORNAY

I0516929

HOW TO GET
100%
BETTER SEX
BETWEEN MARRIED COUPLES

LADIES FIRST!
PLEASE HUSBAND, SLOW DOWN... DO NOT RUSH...
BE PATIENT WITH YOUR DEAR WIFE.

ISBN
978-1-958122-17-4 (Paperback)
978-1-958122-16-7 (eBook)

About the author

Who is Rev. Franck Dumornay?

He was born in a Christian family, first boy after three oldest sisters. His father was a pastor and teacher; his mother a fervent servant of the Lord. She used to encourage her children to read the Bible and she even paid them money to read the Bible, because she knew the power of the word of God to change people's life in any given situation. In one word she wants her children to become a better person. Thank God all of them never left the word of God and the church. In the entire family, God granted Pastor Franck a special favor and chose him. That's why he's so blessed and excited to serve the Lord. **God was never unfaithful to him but he was.** Right now he's leading a church as a pastor. God is great to him and his entire family.

As a Christian man and a pastor, Pastor Dumornay cannot watch pornography, because it's not good for the soul and it makes the Christian feels and looks very dirty before our holy God and sometimes he or she does not feel like praying. It's a disconnection.

Pastor Franck has never been a pervert and now he is still not a pervert either. He's a real man of God, a man of prayer, a church leader, a husband, a wonderful father for his three daughters and a good role model. He is a Christian married man that is living a great life with his family, married only one time, never separated or divorced. To God be the Glory.

So, this is this blessed man that God wants to train and teach couples by utilizing his knowledge and experience.

"How to Get 100 Percent Better Sex between Married Couples" clearly explains in chapter five how to get real sex, great sex. So, get ready to learn, to follow and apply.

Table of Contents

Pastor Franck's expectations from the readers of this "Sex Secret Booklet".

— Young men and women who live together without being married will quickly get married while asking God for forgiveness.

— Married couples who have big differences in their relationships, will, after reading this booklet, become lovely couples while asking God for forgiveness.

— Married couples, who are thinking about separating or divorcing, will quickly become lovely couples again and decide to stay together, while asking God for forgiveness.

— Young man and woman who are enjoying sex without thinking about marrying one day, will finally decide to get married while asking God for forgiveness.

— Young man and woman who are living together that aren't married, young and old couples who have big differences in their relationship, will have a stronger marriage while asking God for forgiveness and accepting him as their personal savior.

— The main goal of my *"Sex Secret Booklet"* is to train and teach every married couple I could possibly reach, to love each other (husband and wife) and more importantly to prove and share their love, like God proved and shared his love to every human being *"But God commendeth his love toward us, in that, while we were yet sinners, Christ died for us."* Romans 5:8 and in John 3:16 *"For God so loved the world, that he gave his only begotten Son, that whosoever believeth in him should not perish, but have everlasting life."*

Jesus is coming soon . . . Are you ready?

Special Thanks To . . .

My dear wife **Yvrose** and my three beautiful daughters, for their support, advice, encouragement and their hard work.

My brother in the Lord, **Randolph Pierce**, and my sister in the Lord **Jeanne Lourdes Dorelus**, for their support, advice and encouragement.

My former teacher and mentor, **Anthony Cherubin**, for his support, advice, and encouragement.

Chapter 1

THE REAL DEFINITION OF MARRIAGE ACCORDING TO THE BIBLE.

Marriage: Legal relationship between husband and wife (a man and a woman).

Marry: When people get married they go through a ceremony in which they promise each other, (the man and the woman), to spend the rest of their lives together.

These definitions are clearly illustrated in 1 Corinthians 7:10-11

> *10 And unto the married I command, [yet] not I, but the Lord, Let not the wife depart from [her] husband:*
>
> *11 But and if she depart, let her remain unmarried, or be reconciled to [her] husband: and let not the husband put away [his] wife.*

If so, it's very important that husband and wife make sure they have a great sexual relationship. According to my personal experience, a married couple that is enjoying a great sex life, has less trouble, less stress, and less conflict in their relationship. However, the couple needs to learn how to create an enjoyable atmosphere and get 100% profit of this experience. I want to help. My *"Sex Secret Booklet"* has everything needed to definitely enjoy a good sex life as a married couple.

Marriage is one of the best institution God ever created.

> *18 And the LORD God said, [It is] not good that the man should be alone; I will make him an help meet for him.*
>
> *21 And the LORD God caused a deep sleep to fall upon Adam, and he slept: and he took one of his ribs, and closed up the flesh instead thereof;*
>
> *22 And the rib, which the LORD God had taken from man, made he a woman, and brought her unto the man.*
>
> *23 And Adam said, This [is] now bone of my bones, and flesh of my flesh: she shall be called Woman, because she was taken out of Man.*
>
> *24 Therefore shall a man leave his father and his mother, and shall cleave unto his wife: and they shall be one flesh.*
>
> *25 And they were both naked, the man and his wife, and were not ashamed.* (Genesis Chapter 2:18, 21-25)

God hates divorce.

> *15 And did not he make one? Yet had he the residue of the spirit.*
>
> *And wherefore one? That he might seek a godly seed. Therefore take heed to your spirit, and let none deal treacherously against the wife of his youth.*
>
> *16 For the LORD, the God of Israel, saith that he hateth putting away: for [one] covereth violence with his garment, saith the LORD of hosts: therefore take heed to your spirit, that ye deal not treacherously.* (Malachi Chapter 2:15-16)

It is frequently reported that the divorce rate in America is 50%. **The institution of marriage is under Satan's attack.** So, let's make more of an effort day after day to keep our marriage going. When a man marries a woman, God blesses them by giving them children. Children are always happy to see their parents have a great relationship. This kind of relationship encourages the children to start thinking about their own marriage also, in the future. On the other hand, if the children see their parents arguing they automatically get scared about marriage.

Listen, **marriage is not an easy thing**, that's why God puts some other distractions in the marriage just to help us stay together. The Sex in the marriage is one of them, the second one after the presence of the Lord between husband and wife.

I'm sure; you already heard those things before: A lady said: *"I will never forget my former boyfriend."* Why this type of statement? Because, she spent a great time with that guy who got the sex secret, and made her over excited, and satisfied. That's why this lady will always remember that guy, who knew how to do things.

This is exactly what I'm going to train and teach you in my *"Sex Secret Booklet"*. Anyone can do it, just get ready to learn, to follow, and to apply. Soon you will be like that guy. You will even be better than that guy. Your name will be changed without the need of a lawyer or attorney. Soon she will call you "honey", "sweetie", "daddy", "baby", "pappy", and so on . . .

You will even get special treatment and attention too. That's what I want to do for you. Train and teach you how to do things, both of you (husband and wife). Read my *"Sex Secret Booklet"* in the morning and practice in the evening.

Before we end this chapter, let me tell you the truth about ladies, they love sex better than money. But not with any guy, so that's why you really need to learn how to do things. I'm ready, and cannot wait to start teaching you. Soon you will be the man. *No more divorce related sex problems*, because you don't know how to have sex and satisfy your wife. Please keep reading, for more exciting information.

"http://divorcerate2011.com/divorce-updates".

Women come first! Men come last!

(Richard Harris)

> It's biblical—Having an active and healthy Sex life, Between Christian Married Couples, is a must, if a couple really wants to be one flesh. *"What? know ye not that he which is joined to an harlot is one body? for two, saith he, shall be one flesh".*(1 Corinthians 6:16)

Chapter 2

HOW TO MANAGE YOUR MARRIAGE ACCORDING TO THE BIBLE?

The Bible says, that husbands should love their wives and that wives love their husbands. Why must the husband be the first to share his love? As the head of the family, he must first show his love to his wife, and then later on, she will give back to him, what she has received from him. So, both will get love. Husband, if you want more love from your wife, give her more, and you will yourself receive more love. The more you give, the more you receive. It's that simple. Soon, you will see other couples approaching you asking for the secret of your loving relationship.

Love is something very important in marriage. Here, I am talking about **true love**. I want you, to read and "MEDITATE" on those following passages in the Bible about love:

—For God so loved the world, that he gave his only begotten Son, that whosoever believeth in him should not perish, but have everlasting life. (John 3:16). Here is God's love for every human being.

-But God commendeth his love toward us, in that, while we were yet sinners, Christ died for us. (Romans 5:8). Please, husband and wife let's give love to each other.

1 Though I speak with the tongues of men and of angels, and have not charity, I am become [as] sounding brass, or a tinkling cymbal.

2 And though I have [the gift of] prophecy, and understand all mysteries, and all knowledge; and though I have all faith, so that I could remove mountains, and have not charity, I am nothing.

3 And though I bestow all my goods to feed [the poor], and though I give my body to be burned, and have not charity, it profiteth me nothing.

4 Charity suffereth long, [and] is kind; charity envieth not; charity vaunteth not itself, is not puffed up,

5 Doth not behave itself unseemly, seeketh not her own, is not easily provoked, thinketh no evil;

6 Rejoiceth not in iniquity, but rejoiceth in the truth;

7 Beareth all things, believeth all things, hopeth all things, endureth all things.

8 Charity never faileth: but whether [there be] prophecies, they shall fail; whether [there be] tongues, they shall cease; whether [there be] knowledge, it shall vanish away.

9 For we know in part, and we prophesy in part.

10 But when that which is perfect is come, then that which is in part shall be done away.

11 When I was a child, I spake as a child, I understood as a child, I thought as a child: but when I became a man, I put away childish things.

> *12 For now we see through a glass, darkly; but then face to face: now I know in part; but then shall I know even as also I am known.*
>
> *13 And now abideth faith, hope, charity, these three; but the greatest of these [is] charity.* (1 Corinthians: 1-13). please reread carefully and meditate on it.

If you really take quality time and slowly read this and meditate on those passages from the bible, I'm pretty sure you now have more love for your wife than before you read those love verses, and let me tell you this you will also receive more love from your wife. Why did it happen like this? Just because you have learned what Love is and now you share more to her so you will automatically receive more love from her also. That means your relationship is growing so you will have a better relationship every day. Soon your marriage will become stronger, healthier, and more enjoyable. Husband and wife will be happy to be together, because:

Better relationship + better communication = better sex.

Then love begins to bloom.

Listen to me carefully, when you get a great sex life between a married couple (husband and wife), you instantly stick together. Everything I've told you, I've been there. You become inseparable that means you will want to be together every moment.

Now let's see together what God wants the married couples to do:

> *22 Wives, submit yourselves unto your own husbands, as unto theLord.*
>
> *23 For the husband is the head of the wife, even as Christ is the head of the church: and he is the saviour of the body.*
>
> *24 Therefore as the church is subject unto Christ, so [let] the wives [be] to their own husbands in every thing.*

25 Husbands, love your wives, even as Christ also loved the church, and gave himself for it;

26 That he might sanctify and cleanse it with the washing of water by the word,

27 That he might present it to himself a glorious church, not having spot, or wrinkle, or any such thing; but that it should be holy and without blemish.

28 So ought men to love their wives as their own bodies. He that loveth his wife loveth himself.

29 For no man ever yet hated his own flesh; but nourisheth and cherisheth it, even as the Lord the church:

30 For we are members of his body, of his flesh, and of his bones.

31 For this cause shall a man leave his father and mother, and shall be joined unto his wife, and they two shall be one flesh.

32 This is a great mystery: but I speak concerning Christ and the church.

33 Nevertheless let every one of you in particular so love his wife even as himself; and the wife [see] that she reverences [her] husband. (Ephesians 5: 22-33).

Please read and meditate carefully on those verses. **I don't want to make any comment about this passage but I prefer to encourage both of you (husband and wife) to read it again and again and meditate on it. Right after the reading, make sure you do what you got to do. Go and apply this to your relationship right away, if you really want to have a great sex life, you soon will be astonished to see how the sex in your relationship is no longer a burden. But a real pleasure for both** of you, without the use of any medication whatsoever (chemicals or naturals). Soon you will shoot me an email laughing, praising God and thanking me for this advice. So, keep doing the good work.

Before we move on, **let's remember God must be the center of your marriage. Love, communication, dialogue, understanding, patience, be humble and open up to each other, always tell each other the truth.** Please do not lie, when you lie you make things extremely complicated to solve, all those are the keys for a successful relationship. Do not worry, if you really want to follow my advice, soon you will get a brand new marriage, (including the great sex you, husband and wife, always wanted so badly).

God is always there to help both of you, husband and wife. Just read with me what He said: *"Come unto me, all [ye] that labour and are heavy laden, and I will give you rest."* (Matthew 11:28).

In Philippians 4:6-7: *"Be careful for nothing; but in everything by prayer and supplication with thanksgiving let your requests be made known unto God. And the peace of God, which passeth all understanding, shall keep your hearts and minds through Christ Jesus."*

In Philippians 4:19: *"But my God shall supply all your need, according to his riches in glory, by Christ Jesus."*

Only God knows why he made you read this booklet God bless both of you. Please keep reading carefully with meditation.

If a couple wishes to get more information to help you better manage your marriage and more importantly your sex life. Please, read carefully the Song of Solomon in the Bible. I hope you will enjoy the reading of these following chapters:

Song of Solomon Chapter 4

> *1 Behold, thou [art] fair, my love; behold, thou [art] fair; thou [hast] doves' eyes within thy locks: thy hair [is] as a flock of goats, that appear from mount Gilead.*

2 Thy teeth [are] like a flock [of sheep that are even] shorn, which came up from the washing; whereof every one bear twins, and none [is] barren among them.

3 Thy lips [are] like a thread of scarlet, and thy speech [is] comely: thy temples [are] like a piece of a pomegranate within thy locks.

4 Thy neck [is] like the tower of David builded for an armoury, whereon there hang a thousand bucklers, all shields of mighty men.

5 Thy two breasts [are] like two young roes that are twins, which feed among the lilies.

6 Until the day break, and the shadows flee away, I will get me to the mountain of myrrh, and to the hill of frankincense.

7 Thou [art] all fair, my love; [there is] no spot in thee.

8 Come with me from Lebanon, [my] spouse, with me from Lebanon: look from the top of Amana, from the top of Shenir and Hermon, from the lions' dens, from the mountains of the leopards.

9 Thou hast ravished my heart, my sister, [my] spouse; thou hast ravished my heart with one of thine eyes, with one chain of thy neck.

10 How fair is thy love, my sister, [my] spouse! how much better is thy love than wine! and the smell of thine ointments than all spices!

11 Thy lips, O [my] spouse, drop [as] the honeycomb: honey and milk [are] under thy tongue; and the smell of thy garments [is] like the smell of Lebanon.

12 A garden inclosed [is] my sister, [my] spouse; a spring shut up, a fountain sealed.

13 Thy plants [are] an orchard of pomegranates, with pleasant fruits; camphire, with spikenard,

14 Spikenard and saffron; calamus and cinnamon, with all trees of frankincense; myrrh and aloes, with all the chief spices:

15 A fountain of gardens, a well of living waters, and streams from Lebanon.

16 Awake, O north wind; and come, thou south; blow upon my garden, [that] the spices thereof may flow out. Let my beloved come into his garden, and eat his pleasant fruits.

Song of Solomon Chapter 5

1 I am come into my garden, my sister, [my] spouse: I have gathered my myrrh with my spice; I have eaten my honeycomb with my honey; I have drunk my wine with my milk: eat, O friends; drink, yea, drink abundantly, O beloved.

2 I sleep, but my heart waketh: [it is] the voice of my beloved that knocketh, [saying], Open to me, my sister, my love, my dove, my undefiled: for my head is filled with dew, [and] my locks with the drops of the night.

3 I have put off my coat; how shall I put it on? I have washed my feet; how shall I defile them?

4 My beloved put in his hand by the hole [of the door], and my bowels were moved for him.

5 I rose up to open to my beloved; and my hands dropped [with] myrrh, and my fingers [with] sweet smelling myrrh, upon the handles of the lock.

6 I opened to my beloved; but my beloved had withdrawn himself, [and] was gone: my soul failed when he spake: I sought him, but I could not find him; I called him, but he gave me no answer.

7 The watchmen that went about the city found me, they smote me, they wounded me; the keepers of the walls took away my veil from me.

8 I charge you, O daughters of Jerusalem, if ye find my beloved, that ye tell him, that I [am] sick of love.

9 What [is] thy beloved more than [another] beloved, O thou fairest among women? what [is] thy beloved more than [another] beloved, that thou dost so charge us?

10 My beloved [is] white and ruddy, the chiefest among ten thousand.

11 His head [is as] the most fine gold, his locks [are] bushy, [and] black as a raven.

12 His eyes [are] as [the eyes] of doves by the rivers of waters, washed with milk, [and] fitly set.

13 His cheeks [are] as a bed of spices, [as] sweet flowers: his lips [like] lilies, dropping sweet smelling myrrh.

14 His hands [are as] gold rings set with the beryl: his belly [is as] bright ivory overlaid [with] sapphires.

15 His legs [are as] pillars of marble, set upon sockets of fine gold: his countenance [is] as Lebanon, excellent as the cedars.

16 His mouth [is] most sweet: yea, he [is] altogether lovely. This [is] my beloved, and this [is] my friend, O daughters of Jerusalem.

Song of Solomon Chapter 6

1 Whither is thy beloved gone, O thou fairest among women? whither is thy beloved turned aside? that we may seek him with thee.

2 My beloved is gone down into his garden, to the beds of spices, to feed in the gardens, and to gather lilies.

3 I [am] my beloved's, and my beloved [is] mine: he feedeth among the lilies.

4 Thou [art] beautiful, O my love, as Tirzah, comely as Jerusalem, terrible as [an army] with banners.

5 Turn away thine eyes from me, for they have overcome me: thy hair [is] as a flock of goats that appear from Gilead.

6 Thy teeth [are] as a flock of sheep which go up from the washing, whereof every one beareth twins, and [there is] not one barren among them.

7 As a piece of a pomegranate [are] thy temples within thy locks.

8 There are threescore queens, and fourscore concubines, and virgins without number.

9 My dove, my undefiled is [but] one; she [is] the [only] one of her mother, she [is] the choice [one] of her that bare her. The daughters saw her, and blessed her; [yea], the queens and the concubines, and they praised her.

10 Who [is] she [that] looketh forth as the morning, fair as the moon, clear as the sun, [and] terrible as [an army] with banners?

11 I went down into the garden of nuts to see the fruits of the valley, [and] to see whether the vine flourished, [and] the pomegranates budded.

12 Or ever I was aware, my soul made me [like] the chariots of Amminadib.

13 Return, return, O Shulamite; return, return, that we may look upon thee. What will ye see in the Shulamite? As it were the company of two armies.

Song of Solomon Chapter 7

1 How beautiful are thy feet with shoes, O prince's daughter! the joints of thy thighs [are] like jewels, the work of the hands of a cunning workman.

2 Thy navel [is like] a round goblet, [which] wanteth not liquor: thy belly [is like] an heap of wheat set about with lilies.

3 Thy two breasts [are] like two young roes [that are] twins.

4 Thy neck [is] as a tower of ivory; thine eyes [like] the fishpools in Heshbon, by the gate of Bathrabbim: thy nose [is] as the tower of Lebanon which looketh toward Damascus.

5 Thine head upon thee [is] like Carmel, and the hair of thine head like purple; the king [is] held in the galleries.

6 How fair and how pleasant art thou, O love, for de- lights!

7 This thy stature is like to a palm tree, and thy breasts to clusters [of grapes].

8 I said, I will go up to the palm tree, I will take hold of the boughs thereof: now also thy breasts shall be as clusters of the vine, and the smell of thy nose like apples;

9 And the roof of thy mouth like the best wine for my beloved, that goeth [down] sweetly, causing the lips of those that are asleep to speak.

10 I [am] my beloved's, and his desire [is] toward me.

11 Come, my beloved, let us go forth into the field; let us lodge in the villages.

12 Let us get up early to the vineyards; let us see if the vine flourish, [whether] the tender grape appear, [and] the pomegranates bud forth: there will I give thee my loves.

13 The mandrakes give a smell, and at our gates [are] all manner of pleasant [fruits], new and old, [which] I have laid up for thee, O my beloved.

It's biblical—having an active and healthy sex life, between Christian married couples, **is a must,** if a couple really wants to be one flesh. *"What? Know ye not that he which is joined to an harlot is one body? for two, saith he, shall be one flesh".* (1 Corinthians 6:16).

Chapter 3

WHEN CAN A MAN AND A WOMAN HAVE SEX ACCORDING TO THE BIBLE?

If a human being despite his imperfections, establish laws and principle to try to do things right. What about **God** who is the **God** of principles and laws?

Do you think that God created this noble institution without any rules, laws and principle? If, this is your opinion, you made a big mistake. Did you ever read, meditate and think about this Bible's verse: *Marriage [is] honourable in all, and the bed undefiled: but whoremongers and adulterers God will judge?* (Hebrews 13:4).

The Bible says: **your body is the temple of God, so you cannot do anything you want with your body, including sex before marriage.** Please, my dear friend read this Bible's passage: *15 Know ye not that your bodies are the members of Christ? shall I then take the members of Christ, and make [them] the members of an harlot? God forbid.*

> *16 What? know ye not that he which is joined to an harlot is one body? for two, saith he, shall be one flesh.*
>
> *17 But he that is joined unto the Lord is one spirit.*
>
> *18 Flee fornication. Every sin that a man doeth is without the body; but he that committeth fornication sinneth against his own body.*

19 What? know ye not that your body is the temple of the Holy Ghost [which is] in you, which ye have of God, and ye are not your own?

20 For ye are bought with a price: therefore glorify God in your body, and in your spirit, which are God's. (1 Corinthians 6: 15-20).

If you feel that this passage has touched your heart, your soul and you want to do something about it, but you just don't know what to do and how to fix this problem with God. Then, listen to me carefully my dear friend, God is love, God loves you so much, that's why he sent his begotten son, his only one to die for us on the cross, to save us and to change our lives. God still loves you, and even if you think you are a sinner, probably a big sinner. Remember, we are all sinners including myself, maybe you are asking yourself right now, if God can save your soul or if God can change your life? My answer to you today is just one word, sure! This is what God is doing every single day in people's lives. He has done that for me and so many others . . . you don't even need to say to yourself "I can't take it anymore" or "I'm tired with life" so on and so on . . . God deeply loves you and even wants to speak to you right now, with a nice and encouraging word just to heal you from the previous mistakes you have made in your life.

Please take a few minutes to read the King David's story in Psalms

51:1-19:

(To the chief Musician, A Psalm of David.)

1 When Nathan the prophet came unto him, after he had gone in to Bathsheba.) Have mercy upon me, O God, according to thy lovingkindness: according unto the multitude of thy tender mercies blot out my transgressions.

2 Wash me throughly from mine iniquity, and cleanse me from my sin.

3 For I acknowledge my transgressions: and my sin [is] ever before me.

4 Against thee, thee only, have I sinned, and done [this] evil in thy sight: that thou mightest be justified when thou speakest, [and] be clear when thou judgest.

5 Behold, I was shapen in iniquity; and in sin did my mother conceive me.

6 Behold, thou desirest truth in the inward parts: and in the hidden [part] thou shalt make me to know wisdom.

7 Purge me with hyssop, and I shall be clean: wash me, and I shall be whiter than snow.

8 Make me to hear joy and gladness; [that] the bones

[which] thou hast broken may rejoice.

9 Hide thy face from my sins, and blot out all mine iniquities.

10 Create in me a clean heart, O God; and renew a right spirit within me.

11 Cast me not away from thy presence; and take not thy holy spirit from me.

12 Restore unto me the joy of thy salvation; and uphold me [with thy] free spirit.

13 [Then] will I teach transgressors thy ways; and sinners shall be converted unto thee.

14 Deliver me from bloodguiltiness, O God, thou God of my salvation: [and] my tongue shall sing aloud of thy righteousness.

15 O Lord, open thou my lips; and my mouth shall shew forth thy praise.

16 For thou desirest not sacrifice; else would I give [it]: thou delightest not in burnt offering.

17 The sacrifices of God [are] a broken spirit: a broken and a contrite heart, O God, thou wilt not despise.

18 Do good in thy good pleasure unto Zion: build thou the walls of Jerusalem.

19 Then shalt thou be pleased with the sacrifices of righteousness, with burnt offering and whole burnt offering: then shall they offer bullocks upon thine altar.

Now, let's read Psalms 32:1-11

[A Psalm] of David, Maschil.)

1 Blessed [is he whose] transgression [is] forgiven, [whose] sin [is] covered.

2 Blessed [is] the man unto whom the LORD imputeth not iniquity, and in whose spirit [there is] no guile.

3 When I kept silence, my bones waxed old through my roaring all the day long.

4 For day and night thy hand was heavy upon me: my moisture is turned into the drought of summer. Selah.

5 I acknowledged my sin unto thee, and mine iniquity have I not hid. I said, I will confess my transgressions unto the LORD; and thou forgavest the iniquity of my sin. Selah.

6 For this shall every one that is godly pray unto thee in a time when thou mayest be found: surely in the floods of great waters they shall not come nigh unto him.

7 Thou [art] my hiding place; thou shalt preserve me from trouble; thou shalt compass me about with songs of deliverance. Selah.

8 I will instruct thee and teach thee in the way which thou shalt go: I will guide thee with mine eye.

9 Be ye not as the horse, [or] as the mule, [which] have no understanding: whose mouth must be held in with bit and bridle, lest they come near unto thee.

10 Many sorrows [shall be] to the wicked: but he that trusteth in the LORD, mercy shall compass him about.

11 Be glad in the LORD, and rejoice, ye righteous: and shout for joy, all [ye that are] upright in heart.

Please my dear friend take your time to read again and again on those passages, after the reading I'm absolutely certain you will feel a bit more comfortable in your body. That's why God's word can do if you let him help you.

20 Behold, I stand at the door, and knock: if any man hear my voice, and open the door, I will come in to him, and will sup with him, and he with me. (Revelation 3:20).

If you want to look for God like Zacchaeus, did God let you reach him and change your life for good? Please take a few seconds to read Zacchaeus's story:

1 And [Jesus] entered and passed through Jericho.

2 And, behold, [there was] a man named Zacchaeus, which was the chief among the publicans, and he was rich.

3 And he sought to see Jesus who he was; and could not for the press, because he was little of stature.

4 And he ran before, and climbed up into a sycomore tree to see him: for he was to pass that [way].

5 And when Jesus came to the place, he looked up, and saw him, and said unto him, Zacchaeus, make haste, and come down; for to day I must abide at thy house.

6 And he made haste, and came down, and received him joyfully.

7 And when they saw [it], they all murmured, saying, That he was gone to be guest with a man that is a sinner.

8 And Zacchaeus stood, and said unto the Lord; Behold, Lord, the half of my goods I give to the poor; and if I have taken any thing from any man by false accusation, I restore [him] fourfold.

9 And Jesus said unto him, This day is salvation come to this house, forsomuch as he also is a son of Abraham.

10 For the Son of man is come to seek and to save that which was lost. (Luke 19:1-10)

Now let's read the calling of Matthew's story:

9 And as Jesus passed forth from thence, he saw a man, named Matthew, sitting at the receipt of custom: and he saith unto him, Follow me. And he arose, and followed him.

10 And it came to pass, as Jesus sat at meat in the house, behold, many publicans and sinners came and sat down with him and his disciples.

11 And when the Pharisees saw [it], they said unto his disciples, Why eateth your Master with publicans and sinners?

12 But when Jesus heard [that], he said unto them, They that be whole need not a physician, but they that are sick.

13 But go ye and learn what [that] meaneth, I will have mercy, and not sacrifice: for I am not come to call the righteous, but sinners to repentance. (Matthew 9:9-13).

My final word in this chapter before I start talking about sex with you: ***"How to Get 100 Percent Better Sex Between Married Couples."*** I want you to stop spending your hard earned money in techniques that don't work and start saving big money, while enjoying 100 percent better sex, sex you ever had before. You have only one thing to do: just tell God I was wrong and I sincerely apologize for what I've done. Please God forgive me and accept me as your child again and He will.

This story of the prodigal son can inspire you, just take a few minutes to read this passage:

11 And he said, A certain man had two sons:

12 And the younger of them said to [his] father, Father, give me the portion of goods that falleth [to me]. And he divided unto them [his] living.

13 And not many days after the younger son gathered all together, and took his journey into a far country, and there wasted his substance with riotous living.

14 And when he had spent all, there arose a mighty famine in that land; and he began to be in want.

15 And he went and joined himself to a citizen of that country; and he sent him into his fields to feed swine.

16 And he would fain have filled his belly with the husks that the swine did eat: and no man gave unto him.

17 And when he came to himself, he said, How many hired servants of my father's have bread enough and to spare, and I perish with hunger!

18 I will arise and go to my father, and will say unto him, Father, I have sinned against heaven, and before thee,

19 And am no more worthy to be called thy son: make me as one of thy hired servants.

20 And he arose, and came to his father. But when he was yet a great way off, his father saw him, and had compassion, and ran, and fell on his neck, and kissed him.

21 And the son said unto him, Father, I have sinned against heaven, and in thy sight, and am no more worthy to be called thy son.

22 But the father said to his servants, Bring forth the best robe, and put [it] on him; and put a ring on his hand, and shoes on [his] feet:

23 And bring hither the fatted calf, and kill [it]; and let us eat, and be merry:

24 For this my son was dead, and is alive again; he was lost, and is found. And they began to be merry. (Luke 15:11–24).

Very nice story and this is the same thing God is about to do for you right now. Please, my dear friend be smart and humble just let God help you, like he did for me before and many others.

God doesn't want to see anyone perish, that's why God put this verse in the Bible, just for me and you: *"The Lord is not slack concerning his promise, as some men count slackness; but is longsuffering to us-ward, not willing that any should perish, but that all should come to repentance."* (2 Peter 3:9).

It's biblical—having an active and healthy sex life, between Christian married couples, **is a must**, if a couple really wants to be one flesh. *"What? know ye not that he which is joined to an harlot is one body? for two, saith he, shall be one flesh".* (1 Corinthians 6:16).

Chapter 4

SEX LIFE STRUGGLES IN THE MARRIAGE RELATIONSHIP.

Finally, we are now ready to start with the sex conversation, we all need to seriously talk about it and you've been waiting for so long. Before we really start talking about sex, real sex with real couples like yours and mine, my dear friend, I want to take a few minutes to let you know, who is Rev. Franck Dumornay.

-First of all—I was born in a Christian family, first boy after three oldest sisters. My father was a Pastor and teacher; my mother a fervent servant of the Lord. She used to encourage us to read the Bible and she even gave us money to do so, because she knows the power of the word of God to change people's life in any given situation. In one word, she always wants her children to become a better person. Thanks to God all of us never left the word of God and the church. In the entire family, God granted me a special favor and chose me to serve him as a Pastor. That's why I'm so blessed and excited to serve him. **He was never unfaithful to me but I was.** He loves me, I love him and I want to serve him, like a slave, for the rest of my life. Right now I'm leading a church as a Pastor. God is great to me and my entire family.

-Second of all—I remember when I was 22 years old, as a young Christian man, I was thinking about getting married, like God wanted it to be in the Bible. With my little experience with the Lord, I talked to myself like this: *"Let me use the power of the word of God to get what I need."* I prayed God like this": *"God you are my father and I know you love me, you knew me before you even put me in my mother's womb. Please,*

God help me get a good Christian woman to marry in a few years." Do you want to know something? God answered my prayer and gave me one of the best Christian women ever! Now we are very close to 2 decades together and in our relationships, God blessed us and gave us 3 beautiful girls. Here is the word I used from the Bible to get what I need:

7 Ask, and it shall be given you; seek, and ye shall find; knock, and it shall be opened unto you

8 For every one that asketh receiveth; and he that seeketh findeth; and to him that knocketh it shall be opened. (Matthew 7:7-8).

So, you can use this for yourself to get what you need from the Lord.

-**Third of all**—When I married my wife Yvrose, she was 26 1/2 years old and I was 28 1/2 years old. She told me that she never had any sexual relationships with any man before and it was the same thing for me too. Just imagine, we were married without any prior sexual experience. Very hard to believe! I know! But it's true and God knows us. Please, my dear friend, try to understand or put yourself in our shoes, how difficult it was for a young married couple without any knowledge in the matter to build a strong relationship. To tell you the truth it was my wife's older brother who got married before us, who told me how to start the sexual relationship process with his little sister. As you already know every beginning is always hard, because you really don't know how to do things. It was a nightmare and a very long journey for us without end. It was a very struggling time in our sexual relationship. Thank God my wife was very supportive, but you know as a human being, some time she lost patience, became angry and wasn't content. I understood her, but what did she want me to do? I really didn't know how to do things. I love my wife and I had a great desire to sexually satisfy her. From there, I started strongly to pray my God who put this wonderful woman in my life. While I was praying God I was also looking for some great information on how to sexually satisfy my wife. I tried so many natural products, but none of them worked for me. My wife and I still continued to suffer a lot. To be honest with you, it was a real shame for me, but I couldn't do anything until God intervened after a lot of years of prayers while we kept trying together to see if we can do better.

Finally, God blessed us, we did it! Amen glory to God! Now my wife and I are ready to share our marvelous experience with as many couples we can possibly reach and are suffering a lot like we were before.

As a Christian man and a Pastor, I cannot watch pornography, because it's not good for the soul and it makes the Christian feels and looks very dirty before our Holy God. When that happened, the Christian don't think about praying because his or her mind is somewhere else. That just disconnects him or her with the Lord.

-Fourth of all—My biggest challenge was to share my experience with my fellow Christians because we used to see Sex as Taboo. In fact, as a Pastor leading a church, I had a hard time to involve my dear wife Yvrose that I love so much and my three girls, church members and some close Christian friends in that enterprise. But at the same time, I really felt that God was pushing me to write my *"Sex Secret Booklet"* and to help a lot of married couples. I'm pretty sure more than 75% of married couples cannot enjoy a great sexual relationship. Just because, they are having sex all the time doesn't mean they know how to get a great and active sexual relationship. That's my main reason I took my time to educate myself first then my family, my church members and some close Christian friends, to show them the "How to". This kind of work is especially a Pastor's job to write a *"Sex Secret Booklet"* to train and to teach couples how to do things.

Let's me give you an example. One day, a Christian married woman in our church came to me and said:

-Can I speak to you privately Pastor?

-Sure! I replied

-Pastor, I have been married to my husband for ten years now, and I never had a great sexual relationship with my husband. He loves me as far as I know and he has no other lady in his life. He's a real Christian

man. But I'm sexually suffering; he cannot satisfy my sexual desires". My question to her, as her Pastor and her spiritual Father was:

-what's the matter my daughter?

She responded:

-Pastor to tell you the truth, my husband is a good Christian man, he loves the Lord and he loves me too, but he just doesn't know how to do things.

-Okay, do you have any kids together? I asked.

-Sure! she said and she continued. *God blessed us with five beautiful children.*

A Little bit surprised I said:

-You have five children together and you're telling me he doesn't know how to sexually satisfying you. I can't believe it!

-Pastor, I understand your reaction, she said. *But, I had ten years of sexual sufferings with my husband. I stayed with him, just because God hates divorce and for the sake of my five children. So Pastor I am fed up, you must do something!!*

Do you think she only needs prayer? Of course not! According to my humble experience, she needs two things:

1. The couple needs to quickly see a specialist (doctor) just to make sure they don't have any medical concerns, and her husband really needs to check his erections. It's always a big shame for any real man who cannot sexually satisfy his wife and this problem needs to be fixed immediately, to avoid any boring relationship or any inevitable divorce).

2. As a real man of God and a real Pastor who really cares about my job, my responsibility in the church is to quickly help her through her situation.

-I'm deeply sorry to hear that, but I will pray for you. I have a question for you my spiritual daughter anyway. I continued.

-Go ahead Pastor! I am really desperate. She said.

-Can I speak to your husband? I asked.

-Sure! She said.

-However, I will need to speak to both of you as soon as possible. This kind of problem needs to be solved quickly, and again as a responsible Pastor I must train and teach both of you on how to do things, especially your husband.

I ended the conversation after taking an appointment with the couple.

Now, Please read this carefully. What I have learned from my struggled sexual relationship is this: *"When a couple has a great and active sex life, the whole relationship will automatically change for the better in a matter of time."* The couple will develop a great harmony with exchange of sweet surnames like daddy, honey, sweetie, pappy, baby and so on. Both of them will even get special attention and will talk about each other with elogious terms.

So get ready to learn from a Christian married man, Sex Expert and Mentor. I really want to train, teach you and change your sex life.

-Lastly—Pastor Franck has never been a pervert and now he's not a pervert either. I am a real man of God, a man of prayer, a church leader, a husband, a wonderful father for my three daughters and a good role model, a Christian married man that is living a great life with my family, married only one time, never separated or divorced. To God be the Glory. So, this is the blessed man that God wants to use his knowledge and experience to train and teach couples with. *"How to Get 100 Percent Better Sex*

Between Married Couples" Real Sex, Great Sex, clearly explains in chapter five of my "*Sex Secret Booklet*". So, get ready to learn, to follow and to apply.

Stop spending your hard earned money and start enjoying Great Sex with your wife! I challenge you, if you really want to learn, follow and apply, my "*Sex Secret Booklet*" could be a miracle for your sexual problems and more importantly your whole relationship will change for the better in a matter of time.

Sexual relationship problem is a serious matter, I've been there before. So be serious about this opportunity God wants to offer you right now through his servant Pastor Franck. Be serious about your sexual relationship to put it back on the right track.

My "*Sex Secret Booklet*" will change your entire life. Soon, you will be happier, healthier, stronger, younger looking and enjoying the best sex you have ever had.

-Read my "*Sex Secret Booklet* "in the morning, apply my advice in the evening, early tomorrow morning you will shoot me an email laughing, praising God and thanking me. To God be the Glory!

It's biblical—having an active and healthy sex life, between Christian married couples, **is a must**, if a couple really wants to be one flesh. "*What? know ye not that he which is joined to an harlot is one body? for two, saith he, shall be one flesh*". (1 Corinthians 6:16).

Chapter 5

HOW TO GET 100 PERCENT BETTER SEX BETWEEN MARRIED COUPLES?

Here's the thing, get ready to learn, to follow, to apply and end your miserable sex life immediately, for the better! You will be happier, healthier and stronger. You'll look younger and will enjoy the Best Sex you ever had. All that, with no pills to swallow, no cream or oil to use and no exercise required. You get my "*Sex Secret Booklet*" and you're good to go. Read it in the morning, practice in the evening and the next morning you will shoot me an email laughing, praising God for this special blessing and thanking me for my "*Sex Secret Booklet*." To God be the Glory!

Learn: how to do something well and even better and better every day. You really need this kind of knowledge, **knowledge = power= money (satisfaction, happiness, life changing . . .)**

Learn: to gain knowledge or a skill

Follow: to be guided by someone who has experience or who knows how to do things. *(You really need to follow someone who's been there before and has great insight to train and teach other people who badly need help).*

Practice: the repetition of an action regularly in order to improve a skill.

Sex between Christian married couples is supported by the Bible So, they need to prioritize it in their marriage, if they really want to see miracles in their union.

Remember SEX is a must for Christian married couples and great sex life is the equivalent of great marriage.

Please, my dear friend read this following sentence carefully; get ready to learn, learn means to me to forget everything you already knew about sexual relationship between couples. Saying this I don't mean you don't know anything about this subject, far from it. I definitely know most of you have great knowledge about this subject, but what I mean is to read my *"Sex Secret Booklet"* and then to practice exactly the way the booklet says to do so. If you want to follow my advice, your sexual relationship between couples will be great in just days, not weeks and your whole marriage will change for the better in a matter of time.

So let's face it, they always said: "**Ladies first**" that's correct. Husbands are gentlemen. In my "**Sex Secret Booklet**" Ladies even come before first.

Let me explain, just be smart my brother I'm talking to you husbands. If you really want to put your wife first, while you are still the head of the family, like God wants it to be in the Bible, do you know what will happen? Soon she (your wife) will put you first too. So, both of you husband and wife will be in the first place. That sounds great! That's what it is. If your wife has a rough character before, now she will automatically become soft and flexible. In other words, you have now a new wife, and the divorce process is terminated. Now there is more joy and happiness in your marriage, less pressure, less stress, and less conflict. It's time now to start the honeymoon. You choose yourself where to take your new wife and probably be ready for a new baby too. Because of too much love . . . Wow!!

Let me say this, the biggest problem in our culture is everyone likes to have sex but nobody knows how to have great sex and nobody wants to talk about sex. We are afraid and even ashamed to talk and to expose our sexual difficulties. Then it makes us uncomfortable to look for help. That's why, we have so many divorces related to sexual relationship problems and married couples always complain, they want sex, they love sex, but they don't really know how to enjoy their sex lives. It's a big problem!

If both of you, husband and wife, want to religiously following my advice, I can surely tell you that today God wants to bless your marriage through my "*Sex Secret Booklet.*"

As a married couple, God wants both of you to fully enjoy your sex life. That's why He created sex, a special pleasure that wife and husband deserve and that will keep their union alive. Period!!

You need to talk about sex all time, if you don't want to talk about sex, you will never get a great sexual relationship in your marriage. Don't be afraid to talk about sex. It's not something nasty and it's not a sin because you are married. God wants both of you to have a great sexual relationship together. Couples who have a great sexual relationship never have time to talk about divorce because they become inseparable; like it is said in the Bible they become one flesh.

Please husbands talk about sex more often with your dear wife. Please wives talk about sex more often to your wonderful husband.

You are legal before God and men; you are married so let's stop the divorce process by talking and having sex any time you want. My brothers don't worry my "*Sex Secret Booklet*" will definitely fix your sexual problem, unless you have a medical problem. If so, you need to quickly visit a specialist to make sure you don't have any medical concerns. Otherwise, read my booklet in the morning and in the evening you will show her now you know how to do things. Just follow my simple step-by-step advice and I am 100 percent confident you will be the man like I am now for my dear wife.

Time to train and teach you the secret. Are you ready? Okay!!

-You only need a minimum relationship with your wife to take her with you to bed. Before that, you really need to talk a little bit about sex with her during the day before you take her to bed with you. That will make the job easier for you. If you're shy, talk to her on the phone or text her and let her know how you are ready to spend a great time with her tonight. Wow! Good idea.

Never forget and always remember
Ladies first . . . Ladies first . . . Ladies first . . .

Ladies always complain about men, when the husband wants to have sex they just come to their wife, they satisfy themselves after that they are gone. They don't care. No, no, no, my dear friend, that's not the right way to do things. My brother, you need to slow down. Please, please, do not rush my dear friend; you will lose your wonderful wife. Someone else who knows the Sex secret will take her from you and you will regret her forever. Do not play my brother you will put yourself in danger and you really need to know how to do things. In a few minutes, I'm going to train and teach you the same way I'm teaching the word of God in my church. So get ready to learn and be the man in demand. My dear brother, you only have just three steps to go to get a great sexual life with your wife:

1. **You need to constantly talk to your wife.**
2. **You need to know when to touch her, what part in your wife's body to touch, to play with and how to start.**
3. **Finally, you need to know my sex secret position, this is the magic one (the critical one).**

Let's get started:

Step one: you need to constantly talk to your dear wife (communication-dialogue) is the key of a great marriage. a) You absolutely need to communicate to your wife. Your wife must be your first and best friend. It's possible, because my wife is my first and best friend and I'm always home with her, if I'm not working or out for something important that both of us have agreed on. Read this carefully, when I want to go to the bathroom I tell her "I am going to the bathroom". Do you want to know something? Our bedroom door is next to the bathroom door. But, this is my way of staying close to my wife like God wants it. When I go to the bank for a deposit, when I came back, I called her, where are you my dear? I showed her the bank slip. We have only one bank account (not two different ones). That's not good for the relationship between husband and wife. There are no secrets between us what so ever. Thank God, I don't have any other lady in my life. God knows me. To God be the Glory! b) We have two ways to communicate and do not be afraid to talk about sex with each other.

1. **Dialogue**—*conversation (both of you need to constantly talk to each other)*
2. **Body language** *You can blow kisses to your wife and you can even talk to her without any sound coming out of your mouth like you are mute. My wife loves body language, because that makes her laugh all the time. You know, laughing is healthy.*

Step two: You need to know when to touch her, what part in your wife's body to touch, to play with and how to start.

It's a real nice game. So get ready to learn to follow and to apply. I'm going to train and teach the both of you (husband and wife) the exact same way I'm teaching the word of God in my church. I always make sure that every church member understands and have no questions before I close the Bible study. Now, let's get started!

Like I said before to you husband you will really need a minimum relationship with your wife. That will make things easier for you to take her to bed. Once, together in bed you (husband) start the conversation. A conversation related to what you're about to do together (Sex). Yes, you have to do it together this way both of you will be completely satisfied. This brief time of the dialogue could be three to five minutes. Right after this brief dialogue, you husband starts the touching. So, what must the husband do? a)Take your wife's closest breast smoothly to your mouth and start playing with it right away. Do not sleep and make sure you give her enough heat through her breast. b) Husband, take your left hand straight to your wife's other breast and start playing with it right away. Please very smoothly, don't be rough, my dear friend. Do not sleep and make sure you play actively and smoothly with your wife's breasts and do your best to give her even more heat she couldn't expect. Soon you will see what will happen to her. You will get great results, believe me. Please, be really patient and don't rush. Always remember Ladies first . . . Ladies first, my dear friend.

It looks like a hard work, in fact it is. But do not worry husband, it will pay off. I've been there. c) This is an exciting step. Please, be focused, follow me carefully and patiently. Thank You.

-Here it is: take your right hand husband, to your wife's vaginal hairs. Please follow me closely. Do not go inside your wife's vagina, your job here husband, is only to play actively and smoothly with your wife's vaginal hairs and very soon you will see what will happen to your dear wife.

Please, be patient. Do not sleep and make sure you give her even more heat that she can't handle. While waiting to see what happens to her. Please make sure husband, to keep playing with your wife's vaginal hairs. Remember: do not get in there, until she asks you personally to get in her vagina.

-Now, the real game is about to start. Please follow me very closely here. Please, please do not listen to her until you are asked to get in there, even if you cannot wait to get in there, to start and finish the game quickly.

-Stop husband, you need to be very careful here. Why? Ladies don't want to end their sexual act like this. They want to fully enjoy this wonderful moment until they become really excited and hot. That will be a good thing for you (husband) and you will see it later.

-Do you remember I told you (husband) do not listen to her? Do you know why? Something greater will happen to your wife, but good for you. Your wife will become too hot and impatient, now she can't wait any longer. So you will see your wife, herself, after your hard work to give her heat, she couldn't even handle, taking your right hand and force it strongly inside her vagina. Congratulations husband!! You're the man!! You got it!!!

-Now the real game starts for her. Remember ladies first. Be patient. Husband, your job here is just to follow your wife's direction. Your wife herself will direct your fingers inside her and she will move your fingers as needed. Soon she will start dancing and crying of great joy. While waiting give her the maximum heat you possibly can and you will be the beneficiary later on. Husband, keep following your wife's direction. Now she's the boss do whatever she wants you to do.

-Husband, give her heat—more heat—more and more heat, until your wife happily asks you to stop, while she is embracing you strongly thanking you and kissing you. A kiss you never had before.

-*"A great sexual relationship between a married couple immediately changes the whole marriage for the better in matter of time."*

Husband, your job is done here, now your wife is ready to work hard for you and give you back what you just did for her. Congratulations once again husband, you did it! I want to tell you that next time will be better and even greater. So, get ready to receive more than what you just gave to her, because now she's so hot and excited. She's ready to share her joy with her new honey, sweetie, daddy, pappy, baby, etc . . .

Step three: Finally, you need to know my "*Sex Secret Position*". This is the critical part—the magical moment.

Let's get started: while your wife is extremely excited. Let me make this clear for you husband, now your wife is a real new born baby, so you can do anything you want with her. Please listen to me carefully and do what I tell you.

Quickly, right after she said to you *"Please, you can stop"* and she takes your hands off her vagina. Please, you husband, lay down on your back on the bed and ask your new wife to come on top of you (face to face and eyes in eyes) while your hard penis goes straight in her vagina. Do not worry, she will take it inside her vagina herself. She needs it because she really needs to continue to enjoy this great sexual moment with her new husband.

-Now, husband and wife need to play together and keep the conversation going, while the two good friends (penis and vagina) are enjoying the game. Very soon, both of you will become so hot and start crying of joy, because of great sexual pleasure. So, both husband and wife are so happy, excited, hugging, kissing each other and the game is over!!!!

-Please never stop talking about Sex together, husband and wife every day, that will keep your wife interested and satisfied, your husband going and even hotter for the next game. Now you can finally enjoy your sexual relationship any time you want and stay excited at all times.

-The same way when you go to church to pray to God and to study the Bible your faith grows. The same exact thing will happen in your sexual relationship, if you want to talk about Sex more often together by keeping the conversation going.

"The more a married couple has Sex, the Better their Sex life will become, the Greater and Stronger their Marriage will become."

Notes

It's biblical, having an active and healthy sex life, between Christian married couples, is a must, if a couple really wants to be one flesh. *"What? know ye not that he which is joined to an harlot is one body? for two, saith he, shall be one flesh".* (1 Corinthians 6:16)

That's why any real couple needs to quickly learn, how to have sex, real sex, great sex, by ordering *"My Sex Secret Booklet"* or by having live counseling. Live counseling with Pastor Franck and your couple (husband and wife) privately.

"Great sexual relationship between husband and wife automatically changes your whole marriage for the better, in a matter of time." Rev. Franck J. Dumornay

Pastor/Bible Teacher
Sex Expert/Consultant

For live and private counseling appointments all over the world... Please Email Pastor Franck at : Fdumornay@aol.com

To get your marriage problems fixed, by the grace of my GOD ALMIGHTY, as quickly as possible....

BISAC Code:

REL095000—Religion / Christianity / Education / Adult
REL019000—Religion / Counseling
REL105000—Religion / Sexuality & Gender Studies

Category: Sexuality/Relationships

Age Level: Adult

Disclaimer: Psychological Advice

Special announcement: Free Marriage Counseling for all couples... All over the world.

Pastor Franck's Marriage Counseling Experiences: in the past two years with our Marriage Organization: "BRIDAL HUMANITARIAN CHARITY" from may 28, 2020 - february 2022 in less than 2 years... By the Grace of God, i made over seven hundreds (700) free marriage counseling for 700 couples of my lovely country people in Haiti ... I can't even count the testimonials from those happy couples... GLORY TO GOD ALMIGHTY now i'm thrilled to make this Special Announcement today *Free Marriage Counseling for all couples All Over the World* through what's app, zoom, direct call ... For Ministries... Churches (men, women and youth associations) we will travel to any where in the world for absolutely free of charge to get your Marriage Counseling done...

My Main Goal before i die, is to bring to my Marvelous God Almighty at very least One (1) Billion Souls in Heaven... Please Holy Spirit help me to get that done... As quickly as possible, for my God's Own Glory, in Jesus Christ Name of Nazareth.

contact information:

Pastor Franck Joseph Dumornay
President Founder and Ceo of our Marriage
Organization: *"BRIDAL HUMANITARIAN CHARITY"*
phone: +19173346956 USA
+19173346956 what's app
email: fdumornay@aol.com
Website : https://pastor-franckdumornay.com/
Facebook: OBHN OFFICIEL
Instagram: Franckjosephdumornay
Twitter: @Franckdumornay